i woke up to God knocking at my door

Cecelia Shine

BookLeaf Publishing

Incia | USA | UK

Presentation by *BookLeaf Publishing*

Web: www.bookleafpub.com

E-mail: info@bookleafpub.com

ISBN: 9789358737738

First edition 2023

To Michelle; to Mia; to Evita; to every teenager who once felt they were missing a piece of who they were always supposed to be.

one heart too many

one day the doctors told my mother i had two
heartbeats. they said this
with a downturned wince and a crinkle between
their brows, like
a sheet of paper which cannot be unwrinkled,
cannot
be made perfect again. when i was born, it was
with
double the blood flow, double the oxygen,
double the fear. when i was
born, my two hearts beat a rhythm that echoed
through my
skull and gave me something to march to, a
hopeful anthem
to keep me going, to keep my bones from
crumbling and
cracking under the weight of my organs, the
overproduced instruments
always humming too loudly, beating too quickly,
working too well. when i was
born, it was with extra love built in; extra love
for gifting neighbors,
gifting mailmen, gifting worms that wash up
when the rain pours down. when i was

born, it was with too many feelings, too many
obstacles,
too many faults. i don't know how my two hearts
are functioning, how their pulse is strong
enough,
suitable enough, for my long limbs, but they
are. they are calling to each other and
answering back, creating a song that
wakes me up in the morning
and then puts me back to sleep
when i need it to. i have two hearts,
and they're surviving and they're thriving
and they're dying one second
at a time, but they're
mine, they're mine.
my god, aren't they
mine?

i woke up to God knocking at my door

i woke up to God knocking at my door
so i curled into my stuffed hippo
and pretended his banging fist
was drops of rain tickling my window

i woke up to God screaming through the walls,
WAKE UP
       WAKE
           UP
OPEN   YOUR DREARY
         EYES
              DO NOT
          IGNORE
        ME
      CHILD
so i stroked my unwashed hair
and hummed myself a little lullaby

i woke up and God was standing at the foot of
my bed, asking
         why do you cry,
child?
          why dont you try
     to stop?

so i sit up and stare him in the glowing eye and
say
this is how i was created, God.
ill stop when you let me

Fruitless

There's this tall
old apple tree
in my back
yard. There's
flower buds
sprouting there,
never blooming;
just existing
to die.
There's a
round wooden
bucket
amongst
branch-shaped
shadows,
waiting to
collect anything
other than
five inches
of non-moving
rain. its
splinter-ridden arcs
have become so
saturated
with silence

that it creaks
itself into sound;
into being.
It stands
stagnant
near my
windowsill,
digging a
dent
through the
mud -- always
empty, always
waiting, waiting
for the tree
to blossom
so it can
provide
fresh fruit
instead of
flower bulbs
missing
their petals.

an ode to Mother Nature's kinsmen

I had a dream the other night I was a bluejay,
and the wind blew
between my feathers like waves through sand.
And when I blinked,
I was high up in the branches of a tree and my
little bird body
had become the body of a squirrel. And I was
soaring over leaves
and bounding across bark in a way I never
thought I could, never
thought I would, and the air filled my lungs in a
way it never had
before, and I could breathe a little easier, and
feel a little easier,
and exist a little easier. And the next time I
opened my eyes,

I was awake in my bed, and my soft brown arms
had returned
to their long scrawny state, a long list of flaws
lining each side.
And the air left my body so swiftly, like it was
there but

I couldn't hold onto it, like I was a ghost and my skin was too
thin to keep the cold out. And I tried so hard to shut off my mind
again, to blink myself to exhaustion so I could be in the clouds,
but the sun beaming through the window was too bright and
too alive on my face, and Mother Nature just wouldn't let me.

The Lonely Tree

branches
tauntingly reaching
overhead, cast silver
shadows
over tired eyes

their withered leaves dance
to the ground and
crumble beneath big
feet bored
of stomping; bored
of solitude

when you fall for the resident straight girl

sometimes when walking through the park
you'll trip and fall over a stick in the mud and a
sliver of wood will bury itself so deep into your
heel that you'll convince

yourself you will never walk again. do you know
what i'm talking about? do you know that pain?
that pain that becomes part of you so that even
when you claw

the thorn out with a pair of tweezers you can still
feel a little hole where your skin used to be, the
kind of pain that floats around in a white sheet,
haunting your

memory so that you can't not remember it. now
every walk through the park is tainted. you can
feel your shoulders being warmed by the sun
like gooey apple

pie and you can smell the morning dew wetting
your sneakers, giving them that ritualistic shine.
but the moisture is making little blades of grass
mold

themselves to your ankles and the tan on the
back of your neck transforms to a scalding red
burn, the skin slowly peeling like a bandaid that
you'd rather

leave stuck to your arm hairs than feel the hurt
of ripping them out, the hurt of plucking
something so embedded in you away from your
body and letting

it ride the wind down to the dirt. maybe you
don't know what i'm talking about, but i know
you know the loss of routine, the changing of
something you adore

with your entire heart and soul into something
that wants nothing to do with you. and even
though you can grit and grind your teeth into
baby powder until

it chokes down the words you can't bare to let
up, she will still see the fireworks in your eyes
every time you look at her and the way you
always spare a

hopeful glance down towards her lips, so soft
and inviting like a bed of rose petals or falling in
love with the resident straight girl.

I cried for losing your face

The Monday morning I lost your photograph,
I cried.
     I cried for your family.   I cried for
your
fuzzy gray cat who couldn't feed itself because
it was born without thumbs.   I cried
for the poems I sent you, collecting dust
in an old crack between oak floorboards.
     I cried for every time you saw my scars
and said they were just as beautiful as
the rest of me. But most importantly,   I cried
for you and that look of wonder you'd give the
moon
everytime it broke through the clouds.   I
cried
for the flowers you'd keep on your windowsill
until the petals turned a rusty brown and
crumbled at the touch of your breath.
     I cried because I missed the coconut-ty
scent
of your hair, how the strands slipped
between my fingers like they belonged there,
like my hands were molded to hold you.
     I cried for all the love I have left, the love
dissipating into the open air,

aimless,
always searching
for a small glimpse
of your smile.

A Poem About Hope

Sometimes hope feels like a ruby
in the red sea, finding fifty dollars on the floor,
a letdown, a drop you on your ass when you
need it the most,
taunt and tease you until you're tired and
yearning for
the moon to rise. will make you want to rip your
teeth out,
will make you want to be a person you're not.
But other times,
a piece of peppermint chocolate on your pillow
case,
will sprout a daffodil outside your front door,
will peek
out of the darkest corners when you never
thought you'd see again
is the reason the sun rises and strangers smile at
you on the train
is the reason the cute boy
from your spanish class saw your scars
and called them beautiful.

will always leave you,
        but will always remember to come
back.

Sometimes

            sometimes
the world
makes you so   lonely
that you can feel the
physicality   of it, the
            hollowness   of your heart.
you can feel the   aging
of your body, the way
  weeds   grow through
your   ribcage, the way
caterpillars make your
            stomach into a   home,
the way a family
of moths   float   up
along your throat to
sing   every   night.
you know that it's   all
part of you, that the
    mites in your eyelashes
belong there like   you
belong   in your mother's
arms. you are   sure
that this feeling
          will pass   just like
all the rest.   you are grateful

to spend time with the
universe   and the universe
is grateful   to spend time
        with you.

Homesickness

falling down a well always ends the same.
the icy dark water ripples over your skin
and the cement bricks leave scratches
on your shins and there, in the sunken
ground, you feel like the only person
left on the entire planet. and you feel
understood. you question if the sky
above you is really gleaming or if
your eyes are creating a shine
that isn't really there. you realize
there's a frog, a little green friend
sitting on a lily pad the color
of your eyes. it's looking into them
like it really knows you, and you wonder
if it really does, and whatever conclusion
you come to will be the right one. and then,
when you're all warm and dry you miss
being cold, you miss the walls so close
around you that cradled you to sleep
every night. and maybe someday,
if you're lucky, you will accept it.
you will accept that life is all sore
muscles and fingers wrinkled up,
and you'll realize that's okay, and
you'll just have to enjoy the company
and the beauty and the well while it lasts.

The Wall

theres a brick wall
standing ten feet high
between me and
my home. the wall
leaves red lines like
claw marks on my arms
when i try to climb over
it, the stone always
too rough on my skin.
birds fly right across
as they sing sweet
songs but their wings
arent strong enough to
carry me with them.
when i try to hit it with a
sledgehammer the
handle breaks into three
smaller chunks and
ladders are just too
damn expensive these
days. one day god will
decide to give me the
strength but until he
does, ill sit here in a
raggedy lawn chair with

a cold beer in my hand,
that yeasty taste on my
tongue. i will not pack up
my things and walk away.
i will not give up on myself
and the house that waits
for me on the other side.

God forgive me

a ghost lived in my house
    when i was younger
and his angry yelps
    soaked through the walls
the same   as his sadness.
sometimes id awake
   to the sound
of a   balled-up fist
pummeling   the atmosphere
and everything would
shake   so suddenly
that crumbs of plaster
   poured down
from the ceiling.

the years   passed
  like trees   blurring
through a car
  window, so the ghost
   in my house
has had   time
to grow up.   his size
  doubled
and   his feelings
  tripled

and   every   last
baby tooth came out.
now a   miniature him
lives inside   of my
   miniature heart.
his screams
    are becoming
my screams
and   his pain
is becoming
        my pain.
and i clench
    my fist
like he always
    did his,   and
my sadness
   soaks   through
the walls.   and   God
  forgive me,
sometimes i see
    a ghost
when i look
     in the mirror.

scarecrow

no matter how fast i run,
or how many fields i clear,
i will always wind up
in the same garden;
arms spread apart
trying to scare
the crows away

When you're a failure

When you're a failure, your alarm clock is noisy
knocking on the door every morning;
one bang after another, is one warning after the
other, you better be up by the time i get
back, I better be able to hear the rustling and
bustling of a teenage girl getting ready
for school or I'll knock again. And
Again. And
Again

When you're a failure, your bedroom floor sinks
under the weight of your feet
while they tiptoe over body bags of past lives,
all rotting memories and old memos
waiting to be forgotten. The junk becomes a
slippery slope of a home and
you're just hoping the ground comes back up
before the sun
does.

When you're a failure, the very knowledge of it
swallows you whole. It follows you
like a dog all day and leaves a sloppy trail of soil
beneath your shoes. It clings

to you like its life depends on it, because it does,
and you swear everyone can
see right through your skin to the rotting flesh
underneath.
You decide that they could never
understand you.

When you're a failure, you're so sure that you're
the only one. You can't swipe away
the fog long enough, can't see clearly enough, to
notice any smog around anyone
else. All you feel are your own two feet beneath
you
and the rhythmic pulse
hiding under your
sleeve.

A little girl's work is never done.

I used to shuck corn
in the Poconos
with my Grandfather.
He'd hold the core still
while my lumpy little fingers
peeled the husks away
from each round
yellow knob.
He'd rip off those
thin golden threads
so that I didn't
get tangled
in them, and he'd
keep the trash bag
open for every
crumpled bit of green
I had to offer.
When we finished
the job, and
all that was left
was a pile
of clean veggies,
my Grandmother
and my Mom

and my Aunt
all cheered for me,
all gave
a standing ovation
for their little girl's
hard work,
and then, when
we were ready,
we'd do it all
again.

in another life...

i am baking a pumpkin pie with my daughter.
we are rolling out the dough,
lining the pan,
filling it up and putting it in the oven.
the crust is uneven and cracked
and dotted with pockets of air,
so the orange surface
sinks down into itself, becomes
concave like my mind has.
she shoves her small face
against the window
and watches the edges brown,
watches bubbles erupt
from the gooey mixture,
watches all those fallen crumbs
turn to dust. she doesn't see
my eyes observing, doesn't see
how they gloss over
like the stove's
clean finish. once she's done,
we are wiping down the counter
and washing dishes in the sink.
we are not sad when the pie comes out ugly;
we eat it anyway, with piles of whipped cream
on top.
our stomachs are as full as our smiles,
and we are the happiest we have ever been.

Biting my Lip Always Helps me Fall Asleep

I knew I wasn't normal when people told me
that blood isn't sweet. It's metallic and tangy
and leaves behind a bitter taste. It isn't meant
to drip down your throat like it does mine,
isn't meant to soothe and refresh you
like strawberry icing on vanilla pound cake,
isn't meant to leave you wanting more.

Blood scares little kids and leaves stains
on your bedsheets. Blood is a deterrent
to all things holy and good. Blood is
the wrecked carcasses of homes, the rubble
that remains after a flood rushes your street.
But for me, blood is different. For me,
blood is the sap that drips from trees
and feeds starving animals. Blood is
the iridescent sheen that coats
oil spills. Blood is the relief
that pours out of you
on a stormy day, and the love
that settles in when the rain clears.

Courage

courage found me in ways I never thought it
would.
courage knocked on my bedroom door to wake
me up
for school in the morning. courage tied my
shoelaces
every time they came undone. courage held my
hand
whenever I cried, handed me tissues when big
bubbles
of snot erupted from my nose like a waterfall of
gloom
and sorrow. courage folded my clothes. courage
tucked
me into bed and waited by my side just in case I
had
nightmares. courage showed up for me when I
couldn't
show up for myself. courage brushed my hair
and took
its time, making sure to be gentle and precise.
courage
pushed me on the swing set and walked with me
under

the summer sun. most of the time I didn't even know
courage was there. it was hiding somewhere inside me,
cowering beneath the ugliness and the fear. it's been in
there since forever, since courage plucked me from my
mother's womb, since my young eyes saw light for the
first time, and it'll be in there until I grow gray hair and
wrinkles and until courage is ready to dig my own grave.

www.ingramcontent.com/pod-product-compliance
Lightning Source LLC
LaVergne TN
LVHW010844200726
843508LV00012B/2745